And the Total Is

by Olivia Hynes
illustrated by Shadra Strickland

 HOUGHTON MIFFLIN BOSTON

Printed in China

ISBN 10: 0-618-90002-0
ISBN 13: 978-0-618-90002-2

8 9 10 11 0940 16 15 14 13

4500432010

Vincent Gates has loved to draw for as long as he can remember. He has notebooks filled with sketches of people, animals, buildings, cars, and cartoon characters. But it wasn't until last Tuesday that Vincent realized that he wanted to become a famous painter!

Last Tuesday was the day that Professor Diggs, an art historian, visited Vincent's fourth-grade class and presented a slide show of famous artists. Vincent mostly liked the paintings that were filled with bright, beautiful colors. His favorites were done by an artist who had the same first name as he did—Vincent Van Gogh.

Vincent Van Gogh had painted amazing, colorful pictures of wheat fields, sunflowers, and starry nights. Vincent Gates wanted to do the exact same thing!

The next morning, Vincent announced, "I'm going to be the Vincent Van Gogh of the twenty-first century."

"How can you be Vincent Van Gogh if you're Vincent Gates?" Vincent's younger sister Willa asked.

"He means that he wants to be a famous painter, like Van Gogh was," Vincent's mother explained. "Am I right, Vincent?"

"Yes!" Vincent replied. "And to become a great painter, I'm going to need some things. Here's my list."

Vincent's mother looked at the list. "Do you think you have enough money for all of this? Oil paints are very expensive and so are many of the other items."

"I have $25.45, and you owe me $4.50 for doing the yard work. I'm practically rich!" Vincent said. "Could you please drop me off at the art shop when you take Willa to her karate class?"

Read·Think·Write If Vincent has $25.45 and his mother gives him $4.50, how much money will he have to spend?

That afternoon, Mrs. Gates drove Vincent to the art shop. "We'll meet you here in an hour," she said.

While Vincent was looking around, he heard, "Welcome to my store. I'm Jeremy Tate. Is there anything I can help you find?"

"Hi," Vincent answered, holding out his list. "I'm looking for these things. I want to be a painter like Vincent Van Gogh. Have you heard of him?"

Mr. Tate smiled. "As a matter of fact, I have. He was a great artist."

"My name is also Vincent and I want to paint just like he did," Vincent added.

Mr. Tate said, "I think it's great that you want to be a painter. I do a little painting myself."

Mr. Tate showed Vincent where he could find the items on his list.

About 15 minutes later, Vincent headed to the counter with the art supplies he had chosen.

Mr. Tate rang up the items and then turned to Vincent. "And the total is $97.75."

Ninety-seven dollars and seventy-five cents! How can it cost that much money? Vincent wondered.

Mr. Tate noticed the startled look on Vincent's face and asked, "Is something wrong?"

"I…I… had no idea art supplies cost so much. I think we have a problem. I've only got $29.95."

Mr. Tate smiled. "Let's go over the list together. Maybe there are some things you don't need yet. After all, you are just starting your painting career, right?"

"I was going to start my painting career, but something tells me I can't afford it."

"Don't give up just yet," Mr. Tate replied, and he started replacing some of Vincent's items with other ones he took from the shelves.

Read·Think·Write How much more money would Vincent need to purchase all the items he brought to the counter?

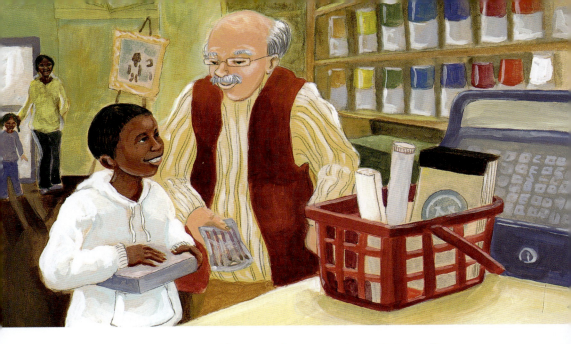

"Okay, let's see what you've got here," Mr. Tate said. "Oil paints are the most expensive paints. You have $53.00 worth of oils. Try these instead—they're called acrylics. They clean up with water. This starter set of 12 colors costs $10.35."

"Also, you have four stretched canvases. They sell for $4.25 each, but you can buy this whole tablet of canvas paper for $5.99."

"Wow!" Vincent exclaimed. "What about brushes?"

"This set of five brushes costs $8.65. Now let's see what the total is," said Mr. Tate.

Read·Think·Write What is the new total without sales tax?

"I think we still have a problem, Mr. Tate," Vincent said. "I don't have enough for this easel. Do you have a cheaper one?"

"Unfortunately, this easel is the cheapest one. Wait a second, though." Mr. Tate disappeared into the back room.

After what seemed like forever, Mr. Tate came out carrying an easel that looked like it could have been used by Vincent Van Gogh himself. Splotches of color covered the entire easel.

"I have had this easel for 40 years," Mr. Tate said. "It was my first easel. Somehow I think it will be in good hands if I give it to you, Vincent."

Vincent smiled. "Thank you! Maybe it will inspire me to create great works of art."

"I'm counting on that. I hope you will share your work with me," Mr. Tate said.

Vincent went to meet his mom.

"Did you find everything?" she asked.

"Even more than I was looking for," Vincent answered with a huge grin.

Read·Think·Write Mr. Tate found items that cost Vincent a total of $24.99. Vincent had $29.95. How much did he have left?

1. The most expensive painting in Mr. Tate's shop sells for $3,000.00. The least expensive painting sells for $19.50. What is the difference in price between the two paintings?

2. Vincent's sister, Willa, wants new karate shoes and a red headband. The shoes sell for $10.50. The headband sells for $3.25. How much money does Willa need to buy both items?

3. Vincent's mother spent $6.50 for Willa's karate lesson, $1.25 for parking, and $11.05 for lunch for three. She had $20.00 in her wallet when she left home today. How much money does she have left?

Activity

Recognize a Main Idea What new activity or hobby would you like to start? Make a list of things you might need to begin your hobby or activity. Next to each item on the list, put what you think the cost might be. Add the cost of the items to arrive at your grand total.